J
513.21
CAV

Cave, Kathryn.

One child, one seed.

For Isis and Makeda — K.C.

Henry Holt and Company, LLC, *Publishers since 1866*
115 West 18th Street, New York, New York 10011
www.henryholt.com

Henry Holt is a registered trademark of Henry Holt and Company, LLC
One Child One Seed copyright © 2002 by Frances Lincoln Ltd.
Text copyright © 2002 by Kathryn Cave
Photographs copyright © 2002 by Oxfam Activities Limited and Gisèle Wulfsohn
All rights reserved.
First published in the United States in 2003 by Henry Holt and Company
Distributed in Canada by H. B. Fenn and Company Ltd.
Originally published in Great Britain in 2002 by Frances Lincoln Ltd.
Library of Congress Cataloging-in-Publication Data
Cave, Kathryn.
One child, one seed: a South African counting book / Kathryn Cave; photographs by Gisèle Wulfsohn.
1. Counting—Juvenile literature. 2. Pumpkin—Juvenile literature. 3. Nkandla (South Africa)—Social life and customs—Juvenile literature.
[1. Nkandla (South Africa)—Social life and customs. 2. South Africa—Social life and customs. 3. Counting. 4. Pumpkin.]
I. Gisèle Wulfsohn, ill. II. Title.
QA113 .C42 2003 513.2'11—dc21 [E] 2002024098

First American Edition—2003 / ISBN 0-8050-7204-7

Printed in Singapore

1 3 5 7 9 10 8 6 4 2

*Oxfam and the publishers would like to thank Nothando and her family, their community in
Nkandla district, KwaZulu Natal, and Kwazi Mazibuko for their enthusiastic support.*

*Oxfam will receive a 5 percent royalty for each copy of this book sold in the U.S.
Oxfam is a Registered Charity no. 202918.*

*Oxfam believes every human being is entitled to a life of dignity and opportunity. Working with others we use our ingenuity,
knowledge, and wealth of experience to make resources and money work harder. From practical work with individuals
through to influencing world policy we aim to enable the world's poorest people to create a future that no longer needs Oxfam.*

ONE CHILD, ONE SEED

A South African Counting Book

Kathryn Cave • *Photographs by* Gisèle Wulfsohn

Henry Holt and Company • *New York*

In Association with Oxfam

1

One child, one seed.

Here is Nothando with
her pumpkin seed.
She lives in South Africa,
where yellow pumpkins
grow all summer long.

*Nothando lives with her aunt Nomusa (in red)
and her grandmother Betty (in blue). Her big
sister and her mother are on the right of the
picture, and her brother is on the left. They live
nearby and spend a lot of time with Nothando.*

Two hands to plant the seed.

Nothando buries the pumpkin seed in the earth. It's November, the beginning of summer in South Africa. The summer rains will help the seed to grow. By February, the pumpkin will be big enough to eat.

The homestead where Nothando lives is in a district called Nkandla. The main house has a kitchen, a living room, and a bedroom.

Its walls (shown in the picture) are made of wood, mud, and grass. They are then plastered and painted. The roof is corrugated iron. Outside, there are three thatched huts called rondavels, which are used for cooking and storage.

Four creatures graze nearby.

All the animals on the homestead have to earn their keep. Cows do that by giving milk. Chicks provide eggs once they're fully grown. When puppies grow up they help keep rats away.

If these cows get too close they'll tread on the little pumpkin plant—or even eat it.

Who will see to it that they don't? Nothando's cousin Mongezi gets that job. He's the family cowherd.

Five friends to pick the pumpkin.

Any month can be harvest time because vegetables grow all year round. Out in the fields and in the vegetable garden you can find cabbage, spinach, beets, potatoes, beans, and mealies (the local name for corn).

The pumpkin's stalk has dried out. That means the pumpkin is ripe. It's time for Nothando and her friends to pick it and carry it home.

Six things to buy.

Sibongile store is a ten-minute walk from the homestead. The town of Nkandla is much farther, and there aren't many more shops there—just a few that sell food or clothes. There's a farmers' market in the town, too.

Now it's time to turn the pumpkin into a feast! Nothando walks to the store to stock up with sugar, mealie meal, bread, margarine, and a passion-fruit drink. The curry powder is for a vegetable curry, tomorrow.

Seven weary walkers.

It's a long walk home for dinner after an afternoon in the vegetable garden. But that's how most people here get around: on foot.

The roads around Nkandla are just dirt, and in the rainy season they can't be used. When the roads are dry, this small van runs a taxi service three times a day from outside Nothando's school into town and back again. The half-hour trip costs six rand (about fifty cents) each way.

The nearest big city is Durban, nearly 200 miles away. Nothando dreams of going there one day.

Eight slices of ripe pumpkin.

Aunt Nomusa adds mealie meal to the cooked pumpkin to thicken it, and sugar to make it sweet. The homestead has no refrigerator, so fresh food has to be cooked and eaten before it goes bad.

Many families can't afford to cook more than once a day, usually in the evening. Those who can afford it often have bean soup or chicken and mealie meal for lunch or a midday snack. Breakfast is usually a mug of tea and some bread.

Tonight Aunt Nomusa is chief cook. Before cutting the pumpkin, she trims off its tough peel. Then she scrapes out the seeds and cuts the pumpkin into slices. It looks a lot smaller now—let's hope there's enough to go around.

10

Ten dinner plates piled high.

It's dinnertime at last. And there's plenty for everyone!

When the meal is over, the children clear away the dishes. They wash up under the cold tap beside the house, scrubbing the plates with their hands or a wet cloth until they are clean again.

The isijingi's gone now, every bit. There's just one part of the pumpkin left. Can you guess what it is?

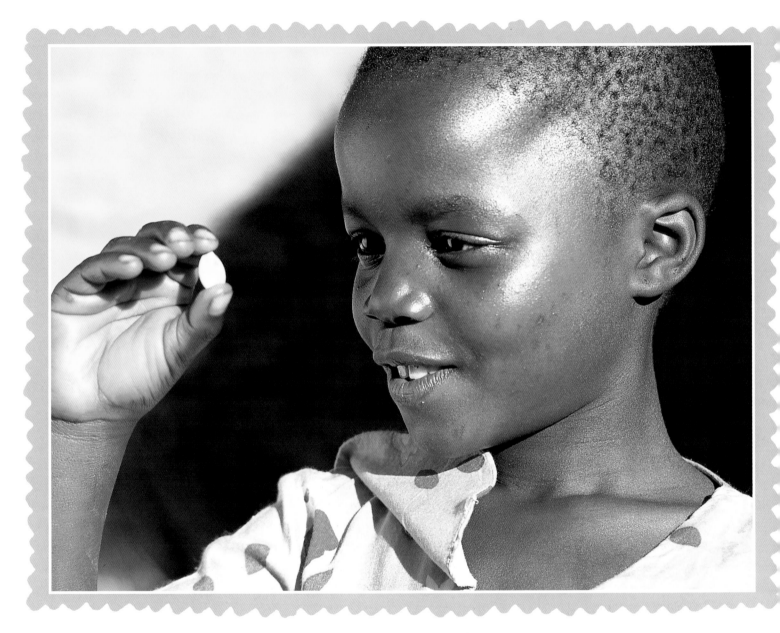

 **1** $\mathcal{One}$ child, one seed to plant next time.

1 one

2 two

3 three

4 four

5 five

6 six

7 seven

8 eight

9 nine

10 ten

More About South Africa

South Africa lies at the southern tip of the great continent of Africa. Nkandla, where Nothando lives, is in the northeast of the country, about fifty miles from the Indian Ocean.

   South Africa is slightly less than twice the size of Texas and over 41 million people live there. The whole continent of Africa measures more than four thousand miles from north to south. The map shows eight of Africa's fifty-four countries.

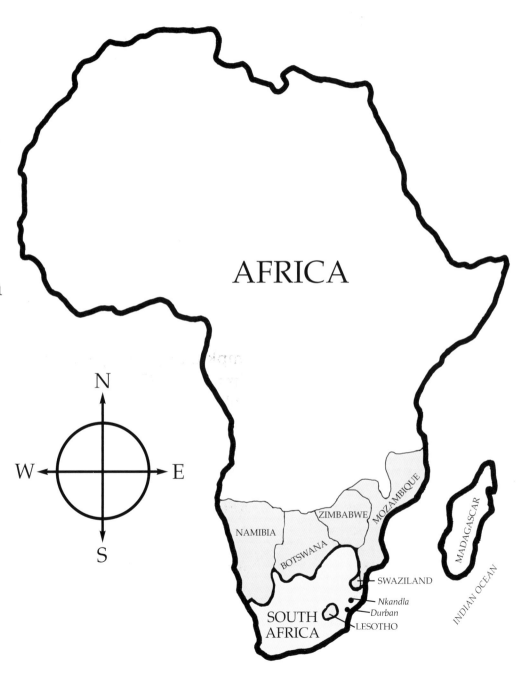

ISIJINGI

This version of the South African dish isijingi is made with ingredients that are easy to find in the United States. It may not look exactly like Aunt Nomusa's, but it is very tasty.

Ingredients

1 small pumpkin or other winter squash (2 to 3 lbs.), peeled, seeded, and cut into chunks
OR 1 15-ounce can pumpkin puree

4 cups water (plus additional if using fresh pumpkin)

1 cup yellow or white cornmeal

1 teaspoon salt

½ cup sugar

Method

1. Place the cut-up fresh pumpkin in a saucepan. Add enough water to cover the pumpkin and bring to a boil. Reduce heat and simmer for 25 minutes or until very tender.
   NOTE: *If using canned pumpkin, skip to step 3, below.*

2. Drain the pumpkin and set aside to cool, then mash with a fork until smooth and free of lumps.

3. Combine 1 cup water, cornmeal, and salt in a bowl.

4. Bring 3 cups water to a boil in a 4-quart pan. Slowly add the cornmeal mixture to the boiling water, stirring constantly.

5. Reduce heat to low and continue cooking until thickened (5 to 10 minutes), stirring constantly to prevent lumps.

6. Mix mashed or canned pumpkin into the cooked cornmeal along with the sugar. Heat through and serve immediately.